the expanded Utter Nonsense

The Poems of Peter Mortimer

Illustrated by Geoff Laws

This edition first published 2001
by IRON Press, 5 Marden Terrace
Cullercoats, North Shields
Northumberland, NE30 4PD
Tel/Fax: 0191-2531901
e-mail: seaboy@freenetname.co.uk
website: www.ironpress.co.uk
Copyright Peter Mortimer & Geoff Laws 2001

The first edition of *Utter Nonsense* appeared in 1977
as a slim pamphlet. It has grown and grown in further prints and editions
in 1978, 1979, 1980, 1986, 1990, & 1993.

Since first publication, many of the poems have been reprinted
in anthologies all over the place

Design and setting by IRON Eye @ IRON Press

Printed by Tyneside Free Press Workshop
5 Charlotte Square, Newcastle upon Tyne

ISBN 0 906228 83 2

IRON Press books are represented by
Signature Book Representation,
Sunhouse
2 Little Peter St
Manchester
M15 4PS
Tel: 0161 834 8767
Fax: 0161 834 8656
e-mail admin@signature-books.co.uk

The Writer

Peter Mortimer
is a prize-winning author in as much as (a) he is an author and (b) he once won a prize at Seely Infant School, Nottingham for blowing out candles. His other gift is prophesy. He has successfully predicted clouds every year since 1967. His Cullercoats terraced house on the North-East coast is famous for plastic bags. Several famous poets have failed to visit there. Occasionally he can be seen on the cliff tops, howking at distant mizzens.

The Artist

Geoff Laws (left)
continues to draw in spite of the "difficulties", and hopes to get it right next time if he can find his pencil. He is still an award-winning cartoonist, and still works partly for *The Journal* newspaper in Newcastle upon Tyne, and partly not.

A Right Royal Foreword

Phillip and I have often been involved with nonsense during our illustrious reign over you all. Only the other day Phillip looked up from his Chinese mufti collection to comment: "Rumour has it, old gel, that you're about to abdicate, and let Chuck stick on the big diamond titfer".
To which I succintly replied: "Nonsense."
As an extremely rich and important person, and one who by necessity must stay somewhat removed from the hoi-polloi, I often find myself in a solitary moment penning the odd nonsense verse.Try this:

A piano fell out of a tree
The politician said, "I see"
It wouldn't win him any votes
So he just took a few notes.

It's rather good, isn't it? In my opinion it has far greater quality than most of Peter Mortimer's poems gathered in this book. I am confident my own collection of nonsense verse would easily outsell this one, which makes it even more baffling why three months on I have failed to elicit a response from Turd Trouser Press of Huddersfield. Am I supposed to include return postage or something?

All poets have to start somewhere. I am no exception.

Now then. The keen-eyed amongst you will have noticed how, during the procession for the latest state opening of parliament, I slipped a nonsensical couplet to Black Rod. I wouldn't claim the old duffer *quite* peed his tights, but it was a close thing - and I speak of a man not given to gratuitous chortling.

Talking of publishers, I confess to having experienced not a little difficulty in getting the sayso to write this foreword. I offered to include a dozen examples of my own work, but to no avail. I also offered several of my own drawings, which again, to my mind, can more than hold their own with the somewhat bizarre squiggles of Geoff Laws (who anyway I see, hails from Blyth). Again, I met with a rebuttal.

Here's another little poem from me:

Billy Bucket
Saw a hen. "Cluck" it
Went. Again and again.

They just come to me you see. You've either got it, or you haven't. That said, I do wish this book well. There is no payment for this foreword, but I am told I receive a few free copies. I intend to wing these to some obscure Royal friends of ours in foreign climes. They should stand Phil and I in good stead for a few invitations. We are, I confess, running out of countries where the locals will patiently stand at the muddy roadside clutching union flags, waiting for us to pass by in a big car.

Oh. Today's Royal Mail includes a communication from Turd Trouser Press of Huddersfield. They have folded.

Consumers' Guide to the Poems

9
Revolting Pets *(at long last!)*
13
Peas on Toast *(the delicacy of tomorrow!)*
15
Bum *(an eternal truth)*
16
Bald Bertie *(look upon him and despair)*
18
Nigel Newlywed *(but for how long?)*
20
Gladys the Tadpole *(beware what you wish for!)*
22
The King and the Hatter *(can riches bring happiness?)*
23
Willy Woanty *(work it out for yourself)*
24
The Woof Pig *(who was around long before Babe!)*
25
Janitor Jeffries *(a thin poem for a thin man)*
27
Babies are Boring *(the rest is propaganda)*
29
Oh Dear *(it could happen - honest!)*
30
Hubroil's Strategic Error *(sponsored by Glaxo)*
31
The Big Fat Plonkerooney *(sponsored by the NUT)*

33
Sid Squidge & The Dinosaur *(forget Jurassic Park)*
42
Tyneside Limericks *(the underrrated poetic form)*
43
Exploding Albertt *(a totally combustible poem)*
45
Pity *(a touch of punny sadness in the book)*
46
Herbert K.W. Tree *(sponsored by London Zoo)*
49
Rogbog the Pig Charmer *(animal metamorphosis)*
51
Great Carrot's Escape from the Munchers *(epic tale)*
53
The Boy Who Mislaid His Vowels etc *(more work for you)*
54
Miss Wobblegob Suet *(fear of flying)*
57
Bigtrousers Dan *(a tailor-made poem)*
58
Herbert the Trouserless Squid *(more trousers! - or not)*
60
Mrs. Chew's Dieting Nightmare *(read, then eat)*
62
Hurray for the Waddle Fish *(much endangered species)*
65
Mr. Humpling the Dumpling's Coat *(read aloud, fast)*
66
Uses for Snot *(a recycling poem)*
67
The Bumtickle Fish *(puzzle poem)*
68
Four Silly Shorts *(the titles are longer than the poems!)*

Also by Peter Mortimer

Stage Plays

Snow White in the Black Lagoon
The Troutbeck Time Traveller
The Man who Played With Mice
Imagine
IT
Elvis Lucy, & Captain Sensible
Doris Dumpling, and the Magic Corner Shop
Dunce Crafty, and the Great Monster Robbery
The Enchanted Pudding
Spirits of the Deep
Whiter than Wight
A Change in the Weather
The Trip
Arthur Raises the Roof
The Nightwatchman
Making Plans for Winkle
Clockman
Lower the Lake!

Poetry

A Rainbow in its Throat

Documentary

The Last of the Hunters
Broke through Britain

Children's Fiction

The Witch & the Maiden
Croak, the King & a Change in the Weather

Revolting Pets

At midnight you could hear them
as they wailed their rallying sound
one million cats in harmony
on the roofs of every town

And word was passed by morning
to marmasets and dogs
goldfish, mice, pedigree ponies
parrots, budgies, frogs

A rattle in the cages
a shaking of flea collars
goldfish banged against their bowls
mice began to holler

On leafy streets and crescents
on suburban avenues
in tower blocks and maisonettes
creatures spread the news

Poodles ran like crazy
leashed owners clinging on
cats whirled and swirled in living rooms
as if all senses gone

Caged birds screeched incessantly
lizards seemed provoked
goldfish flipped and flapped their tails
till Axminsters were soaked

Pets began to wreak
havoc by mid week

Wallpaper ripped off
teapot spouts chipped off
carpets peed on
clean washing weed on
ornaments shattered
jewelry scattered
plants were dug up
(who chewed that rug up?)
sicked-on lawns
missing king prawns
bespoke suits shredded
hydrangeas beheaded
shoes chewed to a leather mess
pillows found featherless
smashed photos in dormers
dogs' noses in kitchen kormas

As song birds squawked for the empty sky
as dogs howled and barked for the unlittered plain
as fish thrashed their tails for clean running rivers
And turtles in Tenby acted insane

Disasters, trauma, dramas,
their owners driven bananas

Until finally the decree:
set all those damned pets free!

Away skipped the dogs from the leash and the kennel
away ran the cats from the tins of mush
away flew the birds from the tinny cages
away slithered snakes to the grass and the bush

Away went Fido and Joe and Polly
and Tyson and Moggy and Cuddles to boot

And Nero and Ginger and Blackie and Topper
with Beauty and Pebbles fast in pursuit.
Away went Foxy and Tiger and Churchill
and Roger and Rover and Benji and Blue
Gandalf and Whistler, Fluffy and Dumbo
Patch, Shep and Shakespeare, and Loopy Loo

And now the cages are empty
the cat food's locked in its tin
pansies grow in the fish tanks
the dog coat's chucked in the bin.

At Crufts the arena's deserted, all leashes and collars lie slack
the pets have gone off to their own place
the pets will never be back.

Peas on Toast

I've seen two legged rabbits
and a bird fly upside down
I've seen a boot made out of glue
and a fish live underground
I've seen peach trees in trousers
and a stone wall dance a jig
heard a walrus recite poetry
and a love song from a pig
many wondrous things I've seen
inland and at the coast
but I've yet to see one person
eating peas on toast

Chorus
Oh please, oh please, oh please
It's what I want the most
let me see one person
eating peas on toast!

I've travelled in a walnut shell
drunk soup that's nine parts mud
I've heard a table cough at noon
worn a waistcoat made of wood
I've tangoed with a donkey
planted flowers with a rifle
I've seen a hat break out in smiles
found live slugs in a trifle
but still my search goes on
I'll not give up the ghost
when can I see someone
eating peas on toast?

Chorus
Oh please, oh please, oh please
it's what I want the most
let me see one person
eating peas on toast!

Bum

Everyone has got a bum
From Nantwich to Peru
Lumberjacks, real docs (and quacks)
Her Royal Highness too

Sweaty wrestlers, scribbling clerks
Jailbirds with tattoed tum
Pale communists, girls rarely kissed
Each one has got a bum

Barbers, bankrupts, one eyed toffs
New orphans rendered mumless
Large ballerinas, red-faced conveners
Just show me one who's bumless

Apart from Norman

Bumless Norman, Bumless Norman
Legs from his neck down to the floor, man
Safe job, warm house, jam tarts with his mum
No bum

He'd suffer the plague, bad breath, lumpy spuds
Confess Hitler was his finest chum
Any sacrifice (not once, but twice)
If he wasn't, minus bum

Norman's glum

Bald Bertie

Bertie was bald, as bald as can be
bald as a light bulb or a freshly shelled pea
as he walked down the street, the kids yelled "Mister!"
"How come your bonce looks just like a blister?"

Chorus (Vivace)
Oh! Oh! Bertie!
And still not thirty!

He applied several lotions, he massaged in cream
he dolloped on potions by the ton- (was *he* keen!)
In a trim-fit wig, revved his new sports coupee
Went too fast with a girl, and off flew his toupee

Chorus
Oh! Oh! Bertie....(etc.)

Spoke to doctors, answered adverts, (alas, none the wiser)
Sweated hours in a greenhouse, smeared his nut with fertiliser
Wrote as *"Anxious, Bognor Regis"*, seeking help from *'Dear Diane'*
thumped his hairy dog called Norman. Grew quite desperate
(like Dan)

Chorus
Oh! Oh! Bertie!....(etc)

Until one day he vanished without no forwarding address
Left one sock and well worn toothbrush, a bed that was a mess
some say that he's in heaven, or very soon will be
but who's that lonely figure in the tight-fitting trilby?

Chorus
Oh! Oh! Bertie!...(etc)

Nigel Newlywed

Nigel Newlywed
took his brand new wife to bed
Oh – that black and shiny hair!
Those rose-red lips and skin so fair!
As for spots – they just weren't there.

(Nigel had come, so calm and cool
to snatch her free of the typing pool)

Thought he; now I do possess her
(like a Volvo – or welsh dresser).
In his yellow striped pyjamas
he felt about as calm as
a dog sat on a nettle
live lobster boiling in a kettle
a dancer, one leg shorter
than the other
"Help – I'm limping mother!"

Listen. Nigel's knees knock like maracas.
I fear he's going crackers.
Casts off a nylon sock
And scarce can stand the shock
of that milk-white rising bosom.
But what's this?
"Er – there was – mmm –
just one thing, I fear
I should mention first my dear . . ."

My sweetmeat my precious
my flower my darling
my scrumptious my dreamboat
my petal my doll
my delight my sugar

my cherry pie, apple of my eye"
(how incredible
he should think her so edible)

"Just there, by your dainty ankle
my very own spouse
is a teeny-weeny
itsy-bitsy
oh so tiny
mouse"
"Aaaaaaaaaaeeeeeeeeeeoooooooowwww!"

Is it so surprizon
she was soon beyond the horizon?
Smiled Nigel/
poor poor poor poor poor thing
she'll be back soon, for me
and for the ring.

Time passes.

Satellites go to Mars
Ford invent new colours for cars.
Vicars munch micro-wave pasties
while digesting video nasties.
And Nigel/
counts the fluff in his belly but
wonders why he's still celibate.
Poor poor poor poor poor thing
(he's still got the ring).

To her own little pillow
In her own little house
A girl whispers nightly
Thank you little mouse

Gladys the Tadpole

This is the tale of a tadpole called Gladys,
who grew up all wrong, (and you know how bad that is).
Life in the pond found her fed-up and yawning,
while all her young friends were busy frog-spawning.

'I want to be a tiger, an elk or ant eater'
said Gladys the tadpole 'life could be sweeter
as a gnu or a buzzard, a giraffe or warthog
anything but a fat slimy frog.

So she packed up a bag and she took to the roads,
away from the lands of the green croaking toads.
She travelled afar, and wore a big floppy hat;
green braces and socks, striped shoes and cravatte.

She learnt how to bark, how to growl, and say 'woof'
She bought four wooden legs , but still not enough.
She took lessons in fighting, and climbing up trees.
'Let me not be a frog!' said Gladys. 'Oh please!'

'Go back to your pond' said a wise hippo called Doris:
'You know there's no place for tadpoles in the forest.
Tadpoles don't fight, build nests or look growly,
they don't play silly games, monthly, daily, or hourly.'

Gladys wouldn't listen, this talk did affront her,
until into the forest came stalking the White Hunter.
Lassoed her legs, locked her up, and what's worse is,
took her back home to be star of the circus.
Poor, poor old Gladys, with her false stripes and fur:
A tadpole gone wrong, what an awful affair!
Now the circus crowds laugh, the audience is joking,
While she leaps through the hoop, (at the same time croaking).

The moral of the tale is easy to spot,
tadpoles should be happy with what they have got.
And white hunters too, even those on the tele,
should put down there guns, eat ice cream and jelly.

The King and the Hatter

There once was a King
who'd never worn a hat
I know what you'll say,
'Just fancy that!
One day in his court,
he thought,
Perhaps I just ought.
So he picked up the 'phone
and rang up a hatter
who wouldn't come at all

'Oh well' said the King
'it doesn't really matter'.

Willy Woanty

Willy
Willy
Willy
Willy
Woanty?

Howdy
Howdy
Howdy
Howdy
Duit?

Hool
Hool
Hool
Hool
Stoppimm?

Woody
Woody
Woody
Woody
D. Sist?

Normal
Normal
Normal
Normal
Sawtit.

The Woof Pig

If you listen hard enough, enough,
you can hear a pig go woof, woof, woof.
Not all the time, just now and then.
There! Was that one?
No. Wrong again.

Janitor Jeffries

Janitor Jeffries
bucket & mops
scrub
polish
wipe
never stops

Janitor Jeffries
cleaning the stair
tiles
steps &
window
in long underwear

Janitor Jeffries
up before dawn
wheeze
cough &
splutter
expression forlorn

Janitor Jeffries
bike in the rain
hills
puddles
splash
'gain and again

Janitor Jeffries
August arrives
on your marks
steady go!
two weeks in St.Ives

Janitor Jeffries
feet in the sea
ice
cream &
winkles
o golly o me

Janitor Jeffries
a fortnight's delight
case
hat &
tickets
back Sunday night

Janitor Jeffries
bucket & mops
scrub
polish
wipe
never stops

Babies are Boring

Babies are boring
(Oh yes they are!)
Don't believe mothers
or a doting papa.
Babies are boring,
their hands and their bellies,
Their pink puffy faces
which wobble like jellies.
Accountants and grandmas
and sailors from Chile
when faced with a baby
act extraordinarily silly.
They grimace and they giggle,
say 'diddle-dum-doo',
they waggle their fingers
(stick their tongues out too).
They slaver and slurp
then they tickle its tummy
they gurgle and drool:
'Oh, he's just like his mummy!'
'Oh, his mouth is like Herbert's!'
'He's got uncle Fred's nose!'
'My word he looks healthy!'
'It's his feed I suppose?'
Save me from baldness
and the old smell of kippers,
but most of all save me
from all gooey nippers.
I'm a brute, I'm a fiend
and no use to implore me
to tickle its chin
because all babies bore me.

Oh Dear

The Government transferred the sea today
said a man in a hat "we'll take it away
the seaside's for all, and not just a few
we'll take it inland and let them have a view".

so now it's all gone, and to fill up the space
they've put factories and flats all over the place
they've pulled down the piers, and wrapped up the sand
and put it in lorries, which hurried inland
In Sheffield and Leeds
They're jumping for joy
at the smell of a briny, the sight of a buoy
and dirty black miners come up for a dip
where once it took hours, on a coach tour day trip

said Mrs McGrumble, who runs a sweet shop
"when they brought in the sea, it was quite a shock
but the man in the hat soon banished our fears
I think I'll get rich, selling cheap souvenires

In Bournemouth and Brighton and Blackpool and Bude
the people consider the action quite rude
and come the election as sure as can be
they'll vote for the party, which will bring back the sea.

Hubroil's Strategic Error

He swallowed the pill
and then felt quite ill.
He should really have read
the label which said:
'All things may follow
if these pills you swallow.
The results will be
most alarming to see'.
And alarming they were,
Hubroil smelt like a sewer.
He grew as fat as a toad,
then as long as a road,
he grew a nose big and hairy
Then wide wings like a fairy.
His skin turned bright blue,
his mouth said 'moo, moo!'
He flew up in the air
the growled like a bear
His hair went corroded
then both legs exploded.
His arms floated away.
His head went the same way!
He bounced of the ground,
and went quite green and round,
until soon he was looking
like an apple for cooking.
'That'll do for me pie'
said a dame who passed by.
And with no further thought,
poor Hubroil was caught.
Sliced up in a pot
and cooked (oh so hot).
He's under the pastry
for acting so hasty

The Big Fat Plonkerooney

At night when you've drunk your Ovaltine
and only black cats and burglars are seen
something happens that's strange, something loony;
out comes the Big Fat Plonkerooney!

The Plonkerooney's special diet
is unique (*wanna try it?*)
The infernal, nocturnal habit
of this creature
is to eat one school teacher
nightly - a mistress or a master
eaten slower or faster
depending on side dish
salad or pasta.
slurp, burp, gobble, munch
and sometimes a leg's saved for lunch.
Maths, science, history,
geogaphy latin or greek
to the Big Fat Plonkerooney
they're all gastronomique.

Though it only swallows (truly!)
those who treat children cruelly.

Examples

Mr Goddard [1], who'd just showered
was straight away devoured

Mrs Cross [2], no question
that she caused some indigestion

Miss Phipps [3], house up for viewing
took a little chewing

Mrs Cook [4], a future head
never - burp! - even left her bed

Mr Smith [5], oh, did I mention?
Gobbled down. So near his pension

Mr Gosden [6], fond of the cane
went to sleep never woke again

****

Private schools, public, junior, comprehensive
the menu's quite extensive.
Not curries, omelettes, mashed spuds or meat pasty
just teachers - who the years have turned nasty.

See that bullying master? Soon he
could be in the tum of the Big Fat Plonkerooney.

1. Geography   2. Maths.   3. Computer Studies   4. French.   5. Biology.   6. History

Sid Squidge and the Dinosaur

Mr and Mrs Squidge, and Sid their son aged eight
lived in Wonkywindy Court, on chips and coffee mate,
tinned peas, tomato pizza, fish fingers and marshmallow.
Mrs Squidge was chubby – Mr Squidge quite sallow.
And Sid Squidge blew big bubbles, from pink sticky gum
And sat around on his bum.

He was bored see? Horribly!

"Pass the salt" said his dad. "Off to bed" said his ma.
"You're spotty" said the budgie. "Ta",
said Sid, "very much".
Dad would come home, and take off his socks
ask, "what's on the box?"
"I don't know why I bother"
moaned his mother.

Quite suddenly, Mrs Squidge went away
"Where to?" asked Sid. His dad said, "holiday"
"You mean", asked Sid,
"without her sun tan cream?"

Poor dad, he rummaged in the 'fridge,
grumbled, "where are you Mrs Squidge?"
"Bloomin' thing"
He ate his fish fingers raw, fried a tin of peas
cooked eggs under the grill, spread sugar on his cheese.
Yuk! Yuk! Yuk! Yuk! Yuk!
Said, "how do you eat this muck?
Bloomin' thing".

When Mrs Squidge came back, she looked very, very well.
Then her tummy started to swell,
and she cleaned the house spick and span

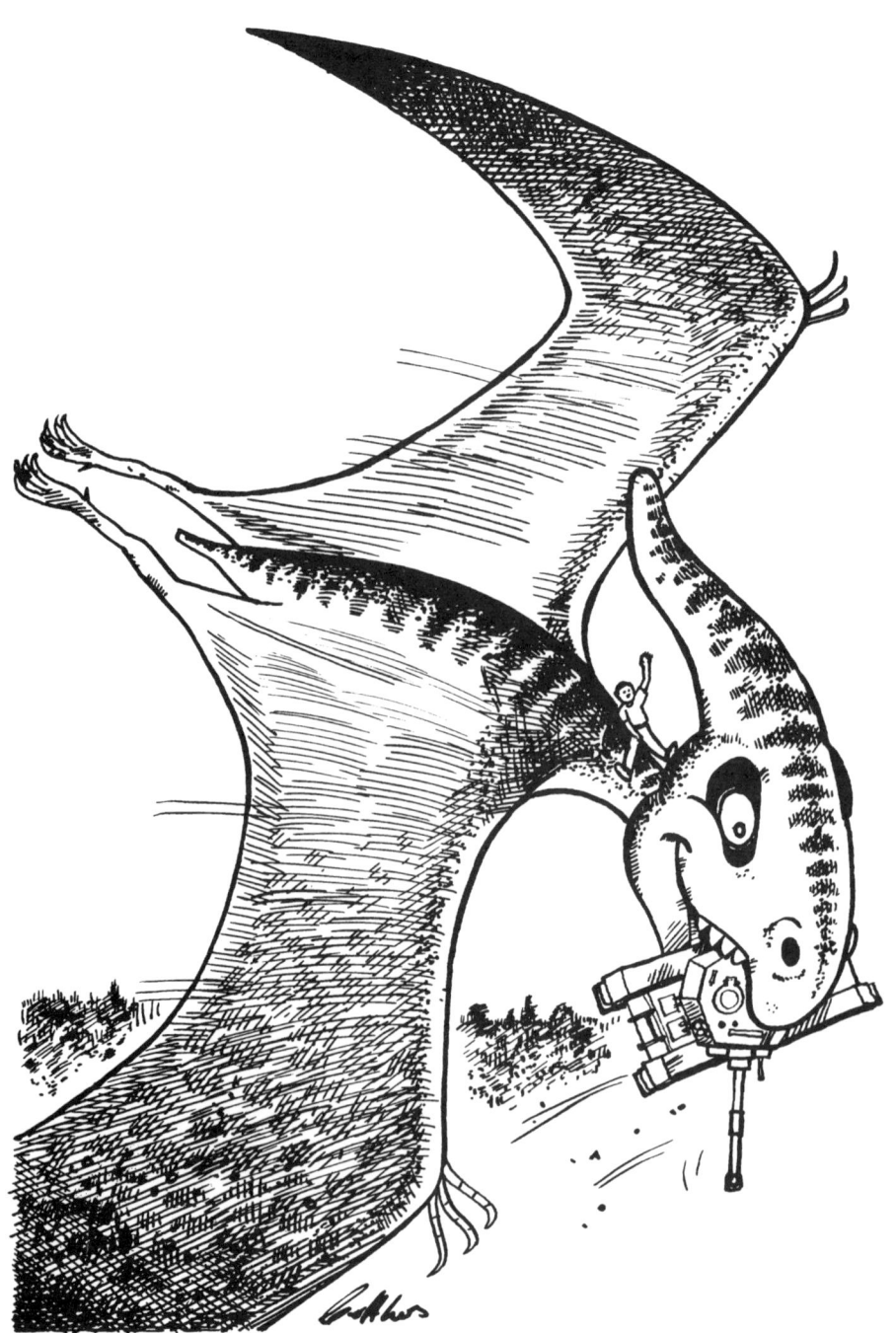

hoover, mops, brush and pan.
Sid asked, "will we have another baby?"
His mum replied, "maybe".
"Hmmm", said dad, while Sid thought he'd rather
have a BMX or ride in a Ford Granada.

He was still bored, see? Horribly!
Then mum went into the hospital with her big fat tum
She came back two days later, but there wasn't just mum!
Sid couldn't believe what he saw -
a baby dinosaur!

Ooochy-cooochy-cooochy-coo!
Diddle-dum-diddledum-diddle-dum-doo!

Sid sang:
"We've got a dinosaur baby
We've got a dinosaur baby
It's a lovely big lump
And its tail goes thump
oh, we've got a dinosaur baby!"

Mr Squidge said:
"I'd prefer a Sharon or a Jason, a Kevin or a Wayne,
a baby dinosaur just doesn't seem the same.
Bloomin' thing".

Sid gave the baby gum, in the pram, out in the hall
and Dino blew a bubble, bigger than a basketball!
While Mrs Squidge got food, strained apricot, creamed rice
which Dino gobbled down - food, jars, top, in a trice!
So Sid wheeled its pram along to the superstore
where Dino ate the shelves, the lino, and the floor.
Cor!

An official man came visiting, said: "For your information
no pets in council flats, it's a statutory regulation"

Imagine the family's faces,
when Dino ate the man's shoes, including the laces!

The police came. Then a magistrate. Then a judge.
Dino wouldn't budge.
By now, it stretched eight foot, from its tail to its snout.
people said "gosh! golly!", when it went out.

And one day, when Dino jumped in the air
it didn't come down – just sort of hovered there.
My, oh my! Dino could fly!
Up on its back with knees gripping tight
went little Sid Squidge, with a fine head for heights.

"Lummy" said his mummy,
staring up at the blue.
"Whatever next? I ask you".

Mr Squidge said "Bloomin' thing".

Up down, round round, and swoop
through the clouds and loop the loop.
Who ever saw
such a thing, as Sid Squidge and his flying dinosaur?

And Sid asked Dino what it wanted to do
Dino replied *"Galumph, galoo! Galumph, galoo!"*
Sid said "I agree with you".
The dinosaur was growing, a mile wide or more
it could digest a double decker, gulp down a cathedral door
It could eat a fleet of taxis, with a hardware shop for afters
It could swallow a terraced house whole, and not choke on/
                                                                    the rafters

Munch, munch, munch, morning noon, and night
What an appetite!

Zinc baths, bed frames, sometimes a dustbin lid
down into Dino's tum, while on his back sat Sid
a'whooping and a'shouting, and cheering on his friend.
Meantime, at the town council, they planned poor Dino's end;
Called up the Air Force, the Army and the Navy.
Mrs Squidge (alarmed) cried, "Hands off my little baby!"
And in a rage, threw stones at a helicopter
Mr Squidge hated violence - so, well, he stopped her.

But the weapons trundled forward, ready for attack
In Dino's ear Sid whispered, and Dino galumphed back
Licked its lips, burped three times, picked its teeth with a maple/
                                                                                            tree
Then tanks came and shot it, fired rounds off, one, two, three

"Fire! Bang! Shoot! Kill!" cried a major mentioned in dispatches
There were colonels, sergeants and corporals with fat moustaches
There were privates, generals, admirals, top brass of every/
                                                                               persuasion
The entire British forces seemed gathered for the occasion

But Dino ate the tanks, then fifteen brand new planes
It gobbled down ten missiles, without any stomach pains
It crunched a few large rockets, it sucked on a gun or two
Its jaws went to work on bullets (bullets were nice to chew)

Galumph, galoo! Galumph, galoo!

And so -
Major General Dombleby Dimbleby Doodah
With a chest full of medals, (a good man in a hoohah)
Planned a new campaign, with his wonderful military brain
Used flags, pins and maps, to make sure that never again
Could a big grinning creature *(galumph, and galoo!)*
Make fun of the army. (It just wouldn't do).
"We shall destroy!"
said Doodah, pressed the button on his newest toy;

A supa-doopa, mega-brill, death-ray computer
technology of the future.
Zap! Zap! Zap! Zap! Zap! Zap!
Deadly power – of this there was no question.
But Dino's roar of pain
was simply indigestion
It would soon start eating again
'cos Dino started to feel
that weapons were its favourite meal.

And with Sid Squidge on its back
having weathered the attack
Dino soared up to the heavens blue,
it was looking for weapons anew.
It had a hunch the French army might be good for lunch
And for tea, why not the air force in Italy?
And the worlds biggest take-away?
Why yes – in the USA!

Mr and Mrs Squidge watched their son head West
"I hope" said Mrs Squidge, "he keeps on his wooly vest.
I mean to say
kids today..."
"Bloomin' thing", said Mr Squidge

Rockets, lasers, aircraft carriers, missiles, & shields that deflect 'em
With just one sniff, Dino's nose could detect 'em.
Weapons and guns, things that spat bullets and flame
Dino gobbled them down – it was such a jolly game!
And in only three days (you'll think this is barmy)
he digested the stock of the whole Spanish army.
Down they went, into that big fat tum
while on its back Sid Squidge blew gum
and thought how, eating weapons all day,
beat maths with Mr Fotheringay
or PE with bullying Mr Smith (all jerks and jumps)
or school dinners where the mashed spuds had lumps

At home watching *News at Ten*
Mum squealed: "It's Sid and Dino again!"
Squeezed her husband's hand in great delight
"Hmmm" said dad, "suppose the lad's done alright"
"Fancy our son being seen
on a telly screen"

And very soon, whole squadrons, platoons, battalions & divisions,
their guns, tanks, bombs, and other ammunitions
began to disappear
in just weeks, not months or a year,
important military places
became great big empty spaces.
An unemployed colonel was left to wave his baton.
A puzzled major could do nothing but take off, & put his hat on.
Soldiers, used to weapon drill,
snoozed, with empty hours to fill.

And governments said: "Because of that fool dinosaur,
we can't prepare for battle any more.
that great big fat prehistoric beast
has left us looking stupid - to say the least.
So now what are we supposed to do?"

Galumph galoo! Galumph galoo! Galumph galoo!

And governments made more weapons, just as fast as they could.
"Yum! Yum!" thought Dino, "they're giving us more food!"
Millions of pounds invested
Chew, gulp, swallow. Quickly digested.

And Sid on the back of his gigantic chum
thought to himself, how the world was plain dumb.
He shouted down to the armies: "As from today
you must settle your rows in a different way,
something that's more fun
than just killing everyone"

Try conkers or marbles, or tortoise races
Or try pillow fights".
Well imagine the armies' faces!
They stomped and they stormed, and they thundered about
you could hear majors bellow, you could hear colonels shout.
They were men trained for fighting, settling things in blood,
But Sid Squidge told them "complaining's no good.
Your weapons are gone, no point building more,
Dino will eat them, just like before!"
Sid spoke true.
And all the experts and leaders said:
"There's nothing we can do!"

Sid Squidge and Dino flew home the very next day
galumphing and galooing almost all of the way
Wonkywindy court was packed full to cheer 'em
Brass bands and bunting, you could hardly get near 'em.
Mrs Squidge in her new hat, welcomed home both her kids
With two mushroom pizzas, (one was Dino's, one was Sid's).
As pretty as a picture, her eyes bright and gleaming;
Mr. Squidge pinched himself, in case he was dreaming.
"Just think" he told the budgie, nibbling at her millet
"The world won't ever be the same. Well it won't, will it?"

And Dino made its home in Wonkywindy park
Became a main attaction, early morning, until dark.
Millions came to see it, on a package holiday
From the lands were all the weapons had simply gone away.
They gave their thanks to Dino, they fed it metal scraps
car bumpers, cookers, bed frames – old cycles and bath taps.

And Sid rode Dino daily, and cuddled his huge friend
soared around the planet, on journeys without end.
Saw mountains, lakes, & forests, but the greatest of all marvels
was the sight of mighty generals
on their knees and playing marbles

Let's hear it for Dino
a one....and a two

Galumph Galoo!
Galumph Galoo!

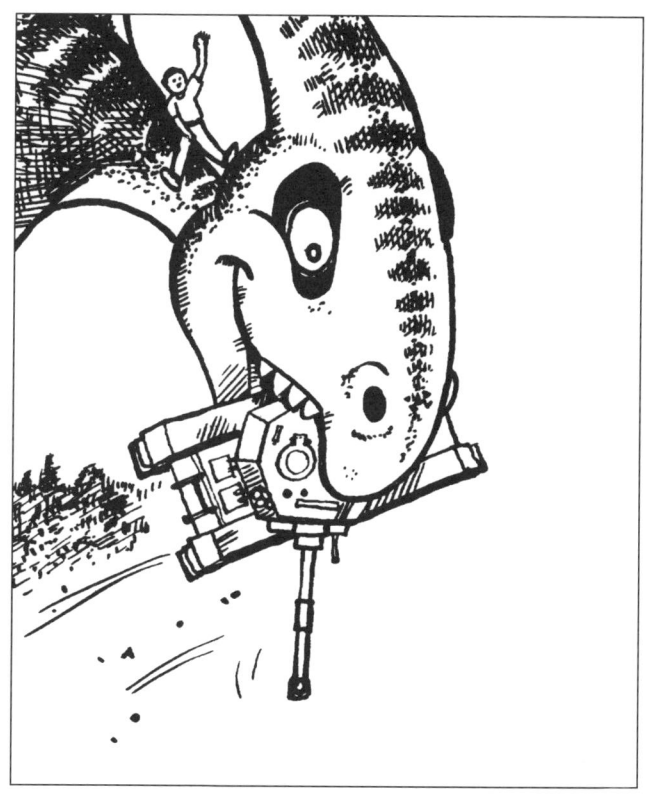

Tyneside Limericks

There was an old dame from Cowgate
who opened a cannibals' fete.
She had hardly spoken
"I declare this fete open!"
when they gobbled her up (and her mate)

*

There was a young lady from Felling
whose tummy just wouldn't stop swelling.
Said the vicar: "You'd better
reveal the begetter!"
But the lady from Felling wasn't telling.

*

There was a young man from Gateshead
who woke up to find he was dead.
He appealed to a judge
but the law wouldn't budge
so he took to the spirits instead

*

There was a young man from Wallsend
who decided to eat his best friend.
He found him quite tasty
but in eating too hasty
he choked on a toe. That's his end.

Exploding Albertt

Exploding Albertt
came into the room.
*Boom, boom, boom,
BOOM! BOOM! BOOM!*
He munched on a grape,
and licked a meringue,
*Bang, bang, bang,
BANG! BANG! BINGUE!*
On the third of the month
and every wet Friday
Albertt exploded
but he was neat and tidy.
'Oh dear and oh gosh'
he'd exclaim with a blush.
'I've gone all to pieces
please hand me a brush'.
He'd sweep himself up
and replace every bit;
He'd stick them on tight
to make sure that they'd fit.

Our Albertt was puzzled,
he scratched at his head.
'Why can't I explode
on a Thursday instead?
Or the fourth of the month
or when it's not raining?'
No-one could tell him,
there seemed no explaining.
Boom, boom went our Albertt,
Boom, boom and *crash wallop*,
his limbs flew in the air
and came down in a dollop.

He exploded so much
(Oh much more than before!)
he blew off the roof,
one window and a door.
'I'm shocked, I'm amazed'
said his auntie called Hortense.
'This time it's too much,
you should really have more sense'.
Albertt checked his diary,
(He was playing a hunch)
it was wet, it was Friday,
and the third of the month.
'That explains it'
boomed Albertt.

Pity

My car broke down
and cried
the day you said goodbye
my toast was all browned off
not understanding why

My carrots were cut up
when you said you'd had enough
I was your little plum
now you think I'm duff

My colander feels drained
My tomato ketchup's shaken
my future looks as lean
as this tasty slice of bacon.

Herbert K.W. Tree

Herbert K.W. Tree
set all the animals free:
Unlocked the cages
(And it didn't take ages)
right there in the zoo.
Look here you,
said a fat nosed judge,
this just won't do,
you can't do that,
I'll tell you flat.
And he banged on the table,
not very nice,
said now I'm able to punish you,
I'll do it in a trice.
Locked him up
and he couldn't get out.
Teach you a lesson
said the judge with a snout.
But it didn't.

Rogbog the Pig Charmer

With a stare and a song and a wave and a blink
Rogbog the Clever could make his pig think
That it wasn't a pig, not a pig at all,
but something quite different, like a hat or a ball.

He could make his pig look like a great ball of stew,
make it jump in the air like a fat kangaroo.
With a twirl of his fingers he could make it conjecture
the likelihood of becoming a movie projector.

Nobody knew how Rogbog could do it,
even magicians said 'we haven't a clue it
seems so amazing, can it truly be thus?'
Rogbog just smiled. Pig miaaawoed like a puss.

Tell us your secret' said the folks, 'we feel thwarted'.
'No' said Rogbog. The pig sat and snorted,
It danced on its nose, its head and its belly,
it jigged and it hopped, and it wobbled like jelly.

Alas for poor Rogbog, he took things too far.
In grabbing the pig one day he said 'ah!'
He stared and he sang and he waved and he blinked
and said to the pig: 'I'll make you something extinct!'

'At the count of fourteen, not one second more,
my pig will believe it's a huge dinosaur.
I'll shock and amaze you, it's my best trick to date'
The crowd jumped to its feet (they just couldn't wait).

1, 2, 3, 4, 5, 6, 7, 8, 9, 10, 11, 12, 13, 14............
The pig made a roar and began gnashing its teeth;
it rose up in the air with the crowd down beneath.

It gobbled and munched and its ears went flip-flap,
its tail hit the ground, and it buried a cat.

'Oh dear! cried Rogbog and he felt his knees tremble
'I never quite thought you would so much resemble
a big slimy monster, please stop it and be
a fat hairy pig again, all soft and cuddly!

Rogbog was too late, too late by a minute,
the people had fled and left him there in it.
Munch munch went the pig and let out a burp.

And ever since then, there's nobody wants t'
meet up with the pig that thinks it's a monster.
They're shouting for Rogbog, and they're sounding so glum.
But they're shouting in vain, 'cos he's in the pig's tum.

Great Carrot's Escape from the Munchers

Men with long noses and some gentlemen of worth
joined in the hunt when he sprang from the earth.
Men who cackled like geese and screeched like a parrot
took to the roads at the escape of Great Carrot.
Great Carrot woke up with a huge yawning sound,
combed his green hair and took a good look around
He rustled his roots, then he shoved and he squeezed
And soon he was free - my, my, was he pleased!

He looked north, he looked south, he looked east and then/
                                                            westerly
but just couldn't decide which route would be besterly.
so he trundled away, oh so big, red and fat,
'till he came to the road and thought : 'Well what is *that?*'
'I don't think I like it' thought Great Carrot, sad and glum,
as he stood by the road, and watched the cars vroom, vroom,/
                                                              vroom.
Into his ear whispered the Vegetable Fairy:
'Go seek out King Beetroot'. And Carrot thought, dare he?

He dared and he did, and went six to the dozen
to the of king Beetroot, (who lived with his cousin).
To the land where a notice - oh - ever so wide
said *'No vegetable here, shall be boiled baked or fried'*.

Where the turnips look happy, and the swedes were delirious
Carrot leapt in the air, (things weren't quite that serious).
He danced on his head, and kissed a sweet pea.
Then bowed to the King (who was having his tea).

In the land of the munchers, they'd begun a search party,
with ten men quite thin, and ten hale and hearty.
They had nets, they had spears, sharp knives and stew pot.
They wanted Great Carrot; sliced up, sizzling hot!

They looked under stones, round corners, and in jellies,
they jumped into dustbins, baby cots & in wellies.
They grew red hot and angry, thumped the ground in despair.
We've lost our Great Carrot. BOO HOO! It's not fair!

For ten years they looked, then 100 years after.
And each year they felt, dafter dafter and dafter.
They all grew long beards, bent backs, curly noses,
bald heads and carbuncles, and hair on their toeses.

In the land of King Beetroot by a gooseberry bush,
sits a smiling great carrot, but quiet please - hush!
He's snoozing and snorting, he's feeling quite dozy.
Even a carrot can find out that life's rosy.

The Boy Who Mislaid His Vowels (inc. 'y') Writes a Note to his Teacher

Pls   xcs   m ,   hv lst ll m vwls.
    thnk   lft thm n th   bs
  t ws   nmbr 68 (thnk)
M   mthr   s vr   pst
M   dd thmpd m
M   sstr jst lghd
Th   gldfsh   s   nhpp
Th   ct wnt   t   ts Whsks
    dnt knw wht   cn d
    wll tr   t   fnd thm ltr
     hv dn m   ggrph   hmwrk
  nd m   mths
  nd m   scnc
  nd m   hstr
Cn   hv sm   mr   vwls pls ?
Pls   xcs m .   m vr   vr   srr .

Miss Wobblegob Suet

Alack and alas for Miss Wobblegob Suet.
She's jumped from a 'plane.
(Said she would do it).

And never did ask what a parachute was.
Never did ask, and the reason's because
only that week Miss Wobblegob had seen
a man bounce in the air from a trampoline.

And there right away she thought men could fly,
and went rushing right off to jump from the sky.
But now poor Miss Wobblegob's falling in flight
and beginning to think that something ain't right.

Lucky for her, there's a lot to be said
For falling five miles, and landing in bed.

(Only dreaming, you see)

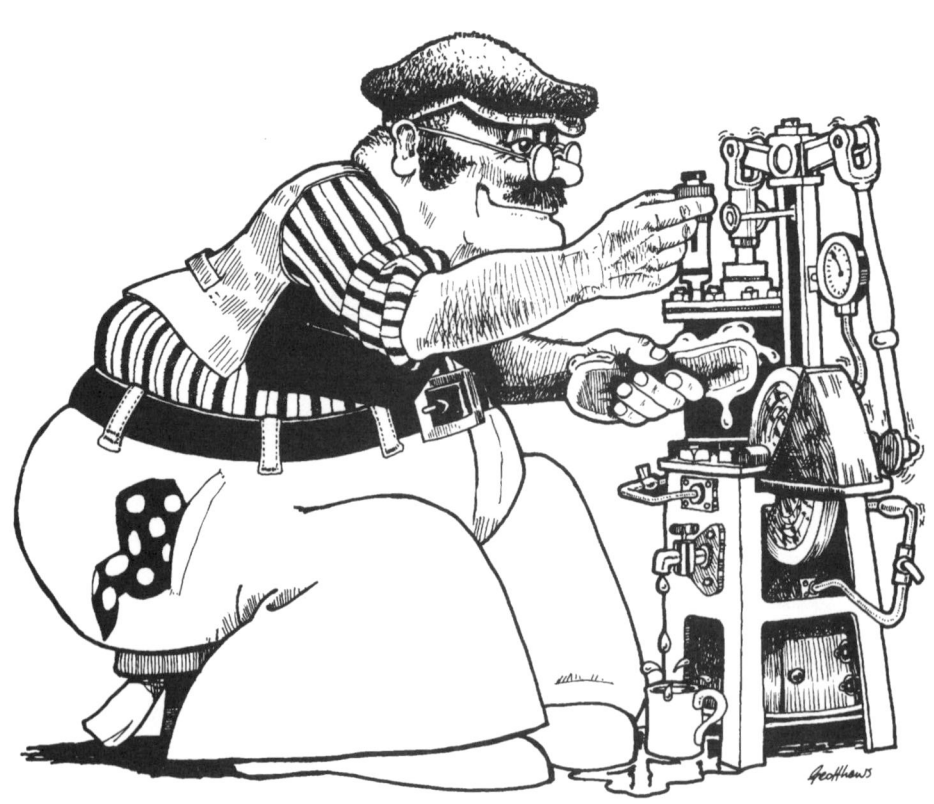

Bigtrousers Dan

In the land of Rumplydoodle
where men eat jollips for tea
and the cows in the hay
feel sleepy all day
there's a wonderful sight to see.
On the banks of the river Bongbong
in a hut made of turnips and cream
sits a whiskery man
name of Bigtrousers Dan
and he plays with his brand new machine.
There are gronfles
and nogglets
and pluffles
and valves go
ker-pling and ker-plang
and a big sugar wheel
that revolves with a squeal
'till it's oiled with a chocolate meringue.
There are wurdlies
and flumdings
and crumchies
that go round as fast as they can
and a marzipan ball
that makes no sound at all
thanks to clever old
Bigtrousers Dan.

Herbert the Trouserless Squid

And o how he hid,
Herbert the trouserless squid.
Blushing he was
and rushing he was
into the seaweed pushing he was
Embarrassed he was
and harassed he was.
O, was he red!

'My name
is shame'
he said.

Looked for some breeks he did,
three long weeks he did.
No trousers to wear
totally bare.
Looking for a tailor he was,
but caught by a sailor he was.
Now he's dressed he is.
Dressed for the best he is.
Caviar and wine sauce,
Herbert's the main course.
He is.

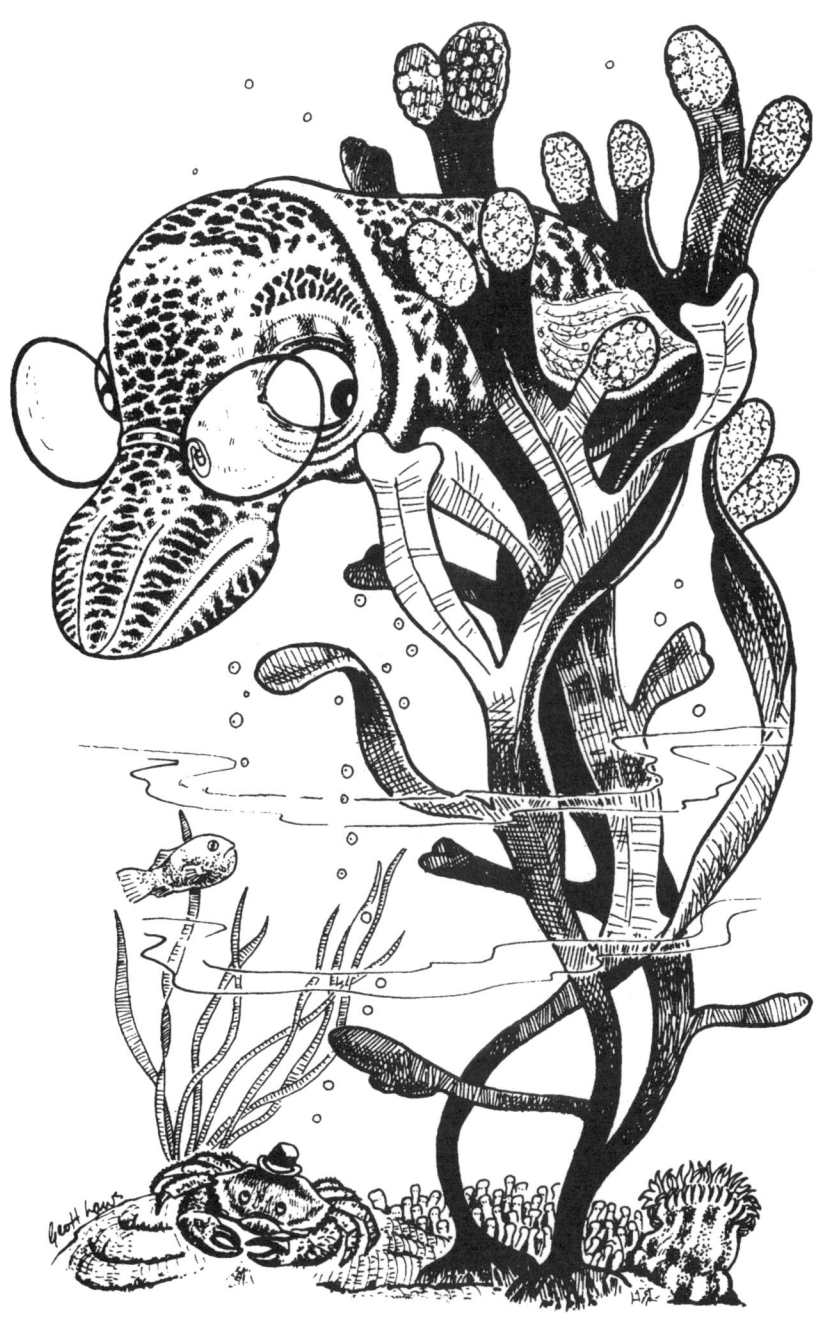

Mrs Chew's Dieting Nightmare

One custard cream she swallowed
and her belt seemed to strain – and then broke
and her thighs seemed the size of two redwoods
from that swig of non-diet Coke.

Without thought she gulped down the red Smartie;
was her bum now a barrel of fat?
And her tum swollen up like a football
from one Mars in the laundromat?

Huge legs, huge arms, huge waistline??
Was that laughter she heard, near and far??
Was she twenty stone, thirty stone, fifty
the result of just *one* Bounty bar??

That dark sin of her late night potato –
was that why her husband had fled?
Could munching those two chocolate biscuits
explain why the budgie was dead?

If she'd only declined that cream gateau
the Cortina might not have broke down
nor both children have turned into monsters
if she'd stuck to the unbuttered brown.

Life was ruined! Who could deny it?
Her inability to diet!
Her husband, children, car, her fate
all linked to polysaturate!

And Mrs Chew made a resolution
she would soon be successful and slim.
She'd allow herself one weekly calorie
digested each Tuesday at ten.

So her body turned into a matchstick
and her legs were two pieces of thread
and her chest was as flat as a mirror
and her neck could scarce hold up her head.

Till she walked down the street like a hairgrip
blown about by the wind and the rain
and then slipped in the gurgling gutter
and was washed like a stick, down the drain
and never was heard of again.

Hurray for the Waddle Fish

When the waddle fish came out of the sea
one hundred people said 'oh my, oh me'.
The Mayor took his hat off and stood on his head.

The town clerk didn't
(Why?)
He stayed in bed.
Over the beach and onto the road
Came the waddle fish, and was *he* like a toad!
(No)

He didn't want popcorn or butter or toast
and rhubarb and custard he didn't want most
of all

Between you and me I think he was clever
to make all those people think, 'well, I never!'

Mister Humpling the Dumpling's Coat

Mister Humpling the Dumpling took his coat to the cleaners
He went back to collect it; the man said, 'I've been as
helpful as I can, but the coat's covered in jelly'.
Thought Mister Humpling the Dumpling: 'That's all very well'. He
took it back home, and scrubbed it with water,
it wouldn't come clean, so he thought that he oughtta
take it abroad to a fat prince or a Rajah
show it a captain, a corporal, a sarge, a
colonel, a major, or some distant ruler,
but nobody listened. They said, 'don't be a fool, the
coat's gone soggy, it's old and it's mouldy'.
Mister Humpling grew sad; with no coat he felt cold. He
wandered about, got his feet wet in rivers,
he sneezed and he snuffled, and he moaned and said: "Give us
a coat, my nose has gone blue, and hear my teeth chatter,
oh give us a coat, a hot drink, a warm hat, a
gas fire and some mustard, a mug of hot liquor.
Don't let me grow cold, don't let me grow sick.' A
long time he wandered, 'till one day on the mountain,
he found an old castle with thick walls and a Count in.
'Come in' said the Count ; 'You are blue, thin, and frozen,
you have ice in you hair, frost on your toes and
you need a nice coat, stewed prunes and suet pudding,
but first wipe your feet, and don't bring the mud in.'
So Mister Humpling got warm, then to his mother he wrote:
'I am living in a castle. There's no jelly on my coat.

Uses For Snot

A flapping shoe sole
is easily secured with snot.
When floods threaten
spread snot along the bottom of doors.
A snot-lined wall insulates perfectly
against neighbours' heavy metal.
Worn-out shock-absorbers on your car?
Fill them with cumfy-cushy snot.
If fired upon by sharp objects
Use snot as a temporary shield.
Add pigmentation to small piles of snot
for an interesting coffee-table display.
Smearing snot on your bicycle frame
protects against corrosion.
Don't spit snot out. Don't swallow it.
Save snot in a plastic container marked *SNOT*.
Secure the lid to prevent caking.
Snot is perfect for hanging wallpaper.

The Bumtickle Fish

I wish, how I wish
that the Bumtickle Fish
would stay out my bath water.
I just think it oughtta

After baked beans or peas
or some similar dish
comes a bathtime visit
from the Bumtickle Fish.

It fires off smelly bubbles
it makes the rudest sound
but in the soapy water
the fish cannot be found.

My mother complains
but oh, how I wish
she'd admit that the blame's
with the Bumtickle Fish.

A Vampire Considers Buying a New Mirror

On
reflection
no

Cardiac Arrest

Have a heart
Constable

Big Noise in Russia

Napoleon
Blown
Apart

Freely Offered Slogan to Car Hire Firm

Love
Hertz